THE TRUE MEANING OF GIVING

Daily December Devotions to Delight Your Soul

Written by Various Authors
Compiled by Lifter Upper

Lifter Upper

GRAND PRAIRIE, TEXAS

Lifter Upper
765 W. Westchester Parkway, #543211
Grand Prairie, TX 75052
www.LifterUpper.com

Scripture quotations marked (NIV) are taken from the Holy Bible, New International Version®, NIV®. Copyright © 1973, 1978, 1984, 2011 by Biblica, Inc.™ Used by permission of Zondervan. All rights reserved worldwide. www.zondervan.com The "NIV" and "New International Version" are trademarks registered in the United States Patent and Trademark Office by Biblica, Inc.™

Scriptures marked (KJV) are taken from the KING JAMES VERSION (KJV): KING JAMES VERSION, public domain

Scriptures marked (WEB) are taken from the THE WORLD ENGLISH BIBLE (WEB): WORLD ENGLISH BIBLE, public domain.

Scripture quotations marked (NLT) are taken from the Holy Bible, New Living Translation, copyright ©1996, 2004, 2015 by Tyndale House Foundation. Used by permission of Tyndale House Publishers, Inc., Carol Stream, Illinois 60188. All rights reserved.

Scripture quotations marked (BSB) are taken from The Holy Bible, Berean Study Bible, BSB Copyright ©2016, 2018 by Bible Hub. Used by Permission. All Rights Reserved Worldwide.

Book Layout © 2019 BookDesignTemplates.com
Cover Photo by Annie Spratt on Unsplash

Cover Design by Kim Steadman, dba Lifter Upper

Developmental Stories Editor, Sharon Rose Gibson: Proofreading, C.L. Burger

The True Meaning of Giving: Daily December Devotions to Delight Your Soul / Anthology. -- 1st ed.
ISBN 978-0-9995457-5-1

This book is dedicated to all the Write More Write Now club members. Your pursuit and love of writing inspires me every day. Remember our adaptation of our theme verse, Proverbs 16:3

Commit and roll to the Lord all your works, deeds and accomplishments. Then your designs, purpose, plans and intentions will be estab-lished, stable, secure and firm.

INTRODUCTION

"What did Granny give to everyone this year?" This was the question on everyone's mind.

When I was a child, the Christmas holidays always meant a trek up the highway to the Ozark mountains of Arkansas. My parents and I took to the hills and clean air to visit with our extended family. Our travel always ended at Granny's little storybook cottage in the pine woods.

On the gathering day, extended family nestled in her snug little home with kids sitting on the floor, adults any place they could sit in the living room or adjacent kitchen. The love between family members was so thick you could cut it with a knife. After we played games like I spy, poor kitty or who has the thimble, Granny's eyes sparkled, and she announced it was time to pass out gifts.

Granny had meager means. Her solution was to purchase all the female family members identical gifts and the males identical gifts, no matter their age. The younger kids would get some candy. Our presents were often a pair of socks or handkerchiefs. By the world's standards, they were small gifts. But, to me, they were the best gifts. Even as a child I knew she was giving the best she had…a gift from her heart.

It is from this story that the topic of this devotional was birthed. As gathering of Christian writers, we wanted to give you a gift from our hearts to yours. We sincerely hope that you feel valued and loved by our simple token and gift from our heart to yours.

Kim Steadman, Lifter Upper

CONTENTS

PART 1: DEVOTIONS

STOP
by C.L. Burger

"After they had heard the king, they went on their way, and the star they had seen when it rose went ahead of them until it stopped over the place where the child was."

Matthew 2:9, NIV

Family gatherings, shopping for gifts, wrapping packages, dashing to the post office, mailing Christmas cards, work parties and baking cookies… and even more cookies.

One word…Stopped.

That is what I wanted. It is what God wanted.

My whole body exhaled.

The Magi got it right. When the star stopped over the place where Jesus was, they stopped too.

Breath held…Holy awe…Silent night.

The sign next to my Christmas tree reminds me. "Jesus is the reason for the season."

The star reminds us to stop.

Exhale…Holy Awe…Silent night.

Thank God, the giver of the best gift…

Jesus

WIND-UP TOYS
by Therese Kay

"She gave this name to the LORD who spoke to her: 'You are the God who sees me,' for she said, 'I have now seen the One who sees me.'"

Genesis 16:13, NIV

Every Christmas morning my sister and I would grab our stockings and run downstairs to open them together with our parents. There was always a gift certificate to the bookstore, a tangerine, candy, a toothbrush and toothpaste (probably to counteract the candy!,) pens, pencils, random doodads and wind-up toys.

The wind-up toys were one of the best parts of our stockings. There was lots of laughter around our wind-up toys as we raced them against each other or watched to see how they moved once wound up.

It wasn't just the amusement of these wind-up toys that was fun and special, but the fact that we felt seen. I can remember almost all the various ones I received throughout the years. I think I may even still have a few of them somewhere.

I remember getting a wind-up turtle when I was little because it was a nickname of mine. When I fell in love with unicorns as a tween, I got a wind-up unicorn. As a teenager, I remember a wind-up telephone - I'm sure you can guess why! My sister who went to an agricultural high school got a wind-up cow. When she became a veterinary assistant, she got a wind-up dog and probably a few other animals. My Dad, who loved reading fantasy books, once got a wind-up dragon.

We only got these toys once a year in our stockings. They were silly little things costing only $2 or $3 apiece but the simple joy, the memories, and the feeling of being seen has lasted my lifetime. It doesn't always take a big or expensive gift to make an impression on someone's life. Rather demonstrate that you know them and see what brings them joy with the gift that you give.

****

Dear God, teach me to really see the people in my life and show them that they are seen and loved.

THE LITTLE WHITE BUNNY
by Debi Flory

"A generous person will prosper; whoever refreshes others will be refreshed."

Proverbs 11:25, NIV

Mom, my little brother, Randy, and I had walked down the street to the dime store to do some holiday shopping. I received $2 for my birthday and was determined to spend it while I was there. I loved the smell of the store. Roasted mixed nuts under the lights, fresh fabric on the rolls, the toys with the "new plastic" smell.

We put some decorations in our basket and walked past the holiday goodies. Randy and I drooled over the chocolate candies sold only during the Christmas season.

Mom's steps were so hurried she didn't notice us stop to admire the stuffed animals. And there it was. A beautiful white bunny with real white rabbit fur, pink crystal eyes, velvety pink inner ears, and a ribbon with flowers around its neck. "Mommy," I screeched, "I want this so much." She told me to check the price tag. I turned the tag over in fear, remembering I only had two dollars. $1.98!

I grabbed it up just as Randy began begging for one too. I promise to pay you back," he begged Mommy. It was so uncharacteristic for him to pay any attention to stuffed animals, let alone desire one so earnestly.

My heart wrenched, seeing his angst. I quietly replaced the bunny and signaled my mom to lean down so I could whisper in her ear. "Please take my money and buy the rabbit for Randy." She pulled back and looked at me with questioning eyes. With a big smile, I nodded my head in confirmation. She instructed me to distract him by strolling through the toys while she checked out.

My heart felt achy because I wanted that bunny so much, but the happiness overshadowed any sadness I felt. I couldn't wait for Christmas.

On Christmas morning, I was so anxious for Randy to open his gift from me; I could hardly pay attention to all of mine. Sure enough, Randy was so deliriously happy my heart burst with joy. He had no idea the bunny was from me.

"Debi," Daddy asked, "aren't you going to open your gifts?"

My heart no longer ached for the bunny because I was filled with joy for my brother. With a smile in my heart, I tore into my first gift. How could this be? Tears of happiness slid down my cheeks as I pulled out an identical bunny from my package. Hugging it to my chest I reached for the tag to see who had given it to me.

To Debi,

When you give from your heart, you give the best gift in the world; the gift of love.

Love, Santa.

UNDERSTANDING GOD'S GIFTS
by Marné Kleinhans

"Now all glory to God, who is able through His mighty power at work within us, to accomplish infinitely more than we might ask or think"

Ephesians 3:20, NLT

As a child, I had dreams of becoming the world's best teacher. I wanted to study in the city and to enrich the lives of many children. My plans were different to those of our Father. In a life-changing series of events, I ended up living on a farm on the outskirts of South-Africa. At first, I couldn't understand why I was in a place where I felt as if I didn't belong.

My heart longed for the city. My mind battled to accept the drastic change of scenery, but our Father knew better. He knew my purpose. Today, I am living the life He intended me to. He gave me a son whose biggest dream is to, one day, become a farmer. I had to move to find my purpose, to raise a farmer who will one day enrich the country by living his ultimate dream.

I asked God for a purpose, He made me a parent.
I asked God to bless me, He gave me a medically complex child.
I asked God to show me the way, He gave me doctors in a different country than where we live.
I asked God to provide my daily needs, He gave me hope, friends, resources and talent.

God does not always give us what we specifically ask for. Sometimes our gifts are disguised as challenges. Overcoming these challenges makes the impact of the gift much greater. It makes us appreciate His deeds more, and help us grow into the person He wants us to be.

Just like a weird looking sweater that serves as a stocking filler, we may not always understand what God gives us at a certain time. We often experience things negatively and question what we are given, but at the end of the day, everything has a purpose.

The greatest blessings in life usually come in forms we don't understand. The odd stocking filler eventually becomes a prized possession in winter. Those situations God gives us which we don't understand, usually becomes the situation we needed. They help us to find our purpose in life, or to realize what He is capable of.

The key to happiness is to accept every gift you receive with gratitude and to believe in the purpose of it. We may not understand the gift, we may not always get what we ask for, but the fact is God knows best. He can give us far more than we could ever ask for.

When looking back, I now realize that I have fulfilled my dream. I am the best teacher in the world — the world of my farmer son.

* * * * * * * *

Heavenly Father, help us to receive each gift in life with gratitude, to see the potential in everything we receive in life. Amen.

CHRISTMAS PAST
Angela's Christmas, Julia Schayer

Angela stood near the door, receiving her Christmas guests. They came straggling in, in twos and threes, some boldly and impudently, some shame-faced and shy, some eager, some indifferent, but all poverty-pinched. Each one was pleasantly welcomed, and passed on to the feast. Angela watched and waited, and at last the door opened slowly to admit old Marg, who stopped short on the threshold, with a look at once stubborn, appealing, suspicious, ashamed. Like a wild animal on the alert for the faintest sign of repulsion or danger, she stood there, but Angela only smiled, proffering her white, soft hand, destitute of jewels, but the hand of a lady.

"A Merry Christmas!" she said brightly.

"I was ugly to ye last night," said old Marg huskily, ignoring the beautiful hand she dared not touch.

"Never mind!" Angela answered sweetly. "You were tired."

"I am a bad old woman!" said old Marg, mistrustfully.

"Never mind that, either!" said Angela. "Let me be your friend. If you will, you shall never be cold or hungry again."

A profound wonder came into the old face— then it began to writhe, and from each eye oozed scant tears, seeking a channel amid the seams and wrinkles of the sunken cheeks.

"You will let me be your friend," urged Angela.

Still old Marg wept silently, the scant tears of age.

"You shall have a pleasant home and———"

A swift, suspicious glance darted from the wet eyes.

"Not a 'sylum, miss, please!" said the old woman.

"No," said Angela quietly. "Not an asylum, A home—a bright, clean, comfortable home———"

"I can work, miss!" put in old Marg, doubling her knotted hands to show their strength. "I can wash, an' scrub——"

"Yes," said Angela, "you may work all you are able, helping to keep things clean and comfortable."

Still old Marg looked doubtful. Wiping her cheeks with a corner of the shawl, she half turned toward the door.

"Have you a family, or any one belonging to you?" asked Angela, thinking to have reached the root of the difficulty.

"Yes," said the old woman stoutly. "I have a cat. Where I go, she must go, too!"

Angela patted the grimy hand, with a laugh which was good to hear.

"I understand you perfectly," she said. "I have a cat of my own. You and *your* cat shall not be separated."

An excerpt from the book A <u>Budget of Christmas Tales by Charles Dickens and others</u>, copyright 1895

****

Dear Lord, Please remind me to be mindful of those around me. Let me see beyond their gruff exterior and to connect with the hearts of your people. Amen.

THE GIFT OF BELONGING
by Kathleen Schwab

"The King will reply, 'Truly I tell you, whatever you did for one of the least of these brothers and sisters of mine, you did for me.'"

Matthew 25:40, NIV

"I have something going on." Just the tone made everyone hold their breath. During a leadership meeting, she continued, "I just found out that I'm pregnant, and my husband is really upset. He says if I don't get an abortion, he's going to divorce me." She was, of course, financially supported by him. Besides, he made it clear he would fight for custody of their toddler and teenager if she didn't do what he wanted.

Twenty years ago, I was co-leading a group called MOPS, which stands for Mothers of Pre-Schoolers. MOPS is a great ministry for mothers of small children, a chance to get a small break and connect with other women. I looked forward to a year of crafts, day trips, and fun. When things took a serious turn, God asked more from us.

What can you give a person facing this kind of crisis? Over the next eight months, our group gave something very valuable in this modern, rushed world, a place to belong.

Maybe because the troubles facing her were so big, and so outside of anyone's ability to control, the group did not burden her with advice. No one tried to tell her what to do or analyze her or the situation. Instead, we listened and prayed. She came to every meeting, and pitched in with all the work of planning, setting up, and breaking down. The others on the team would ask after her home life, and she would update us.

She fought a long, quiet battle for her family, asking her husband not to move out when he insisted he was going to. She didn't move out herself when he demanded it, and continued to keep the household running. Sometimes she needed listeners, but more often, she just wanted to be a part of a group.

In the end, her husband neither left nor filed for divorce. Once his son arrived, the father left all his doubts behind him, and they moved on from there.

I've thought about this whole situation many times over the years, because I think what the group gave during that time is rare. If you look around at social media, television, and church services, you see plenty of lectures and advice. Opinions are everywhere, yet meaningful connection is hard to come by. A group that will accept and include you, even while your life is unraveling, is precious.

Loneliness and isolation are epidemic in our times. No matter who you are, you can offer this gift of belonging to other people. The opportunities are endless. And whenever you reach out to include others, you are including Jesus, too.

* * * * * * * *

Dear God, please help me to see those around me who need the gift of belonging and to offer them the community they need. Amen.

THE GIFT OF FORGIVENESS
by Debra Madden

"bearing with one another, and forgiving each other, if any man has a complaint against any; even as Christ forgave you, so you also do."

Colossians 3:13, WEB

I got home from a church concert, when my husband said, "You better sit down. I have something to tell you." A little worried, I sat down to listen. He said, "I got a call tonight from your brother and you have a sister. Confused and shocked, I sat there in disbelief. All kinds of emotions flooded my heart. He said, "She is a full sister."

I couldn't wait to talk to her. I had so many questions. We talked on the phone and made plans to meet.

I flew to my brother's house in Florida, to meet my sister for the first time. We got to see each other a few times after that, and we talked on the phone until all hours of the night. On one occasion, she said some things, which hurt me. I didn't talk to her for a while. Then I found out she had cancer. By the time I found this out, she was near the end. It was by God's grace that I got to go see her and make things right with her. I stayed with her in the hospice until she took her last breath. I now live with the regret. Because of unforgiveness, I wasted time we could have had together.

We have all been hurt and forgiveness is not an easy gift to give, but God tells us in his word to forgive. I am sure some of you reading this right now may think; *you do not understand how deeply I have been hurt.* You are right, I don't know your story. But I know that God would never ask us to do anything that he did not give us the strength and power to do.

Unforgiveness affects every area of our relationship with God and our lives. We lose our connection in prayer with God; we lose our peace. We replay the hurt over and over, and it affects the way we receive from the person who hurt us. Unforgiveness also affects how we interact with our other relationships. We receive what they say or do from a place of hurt. Unforgiveness also affects our health. Many people go to their graves with anger in their heart.

Don't miss the blessings of God for your life. Right now at this very moment with God's help, you can give that gift of forgiveness and totally set yourself free. Don't let that hurt control your life any longer. Let it go, give it to God. You just need to let go, and he will meet you right where you are.

* * * * * * * *

*Father, please give us your strength and power
to forgive. Help us to see the peace and freedom
we gain when we forgive those that hurt us.
Help us to love as if we were never offended.
Amen.*

SHARING WITH OTHERS
by Anonymous Author

"But don't forget to be doing good and sharing, for with such sacrifices God is well pleased."

Hebrews 13:16, WEB

Bryan was in the fourth grade when a severe car accident injured his dad. He survived, but he wasn't able to work. He had a long road to recovery ahead that would include multiple surgeries and months of physical therapy.

Overnight, Bryan's life changed. His mom started working long hours, trying to keep a roof over their heads. As the Christmas season neared, the Christmas tree went up but there were no gifts under it.

Bryan's older brother explained that there wasn't enough money to go around. "We'll have Dad and that's the best gift," as his brother comforted him.

A few days before Christmas, there was a knock on the door. When Bryan's mom opened it, an older man introduced himself. He explained that he was from a local organization and they wanted to provide Christmas for the family. Laying at his feet were sacks of groceries, gift baskets of delicious treats, a few presents for the family, and two huge, billowing poinsettia plants—his mom's favorite Christmas decoration.

Years later, Bryan still remembers that as his best Christmas. Not because of the gifts but because it meant neighbors had not forgotten his family. Now Bryan saves up year round to afford gifts for other families in need. He wants them to know that God sees their situation and cares.

* * * * * * * *

God, please show me a family I could bless this Christmas. I want to be part of comforting families like Bryan's this holiday season.

GOD'S WISH LIST
by Valerie Riese

> *"Therefore, let us offer through Jesus a continual sacrifice of praise to God, proclaiming our allegiance to his name."*
>
> *Hebrews 13:15, NLT*

My in-laws find great joy in showering their loved ones with gifts during Christmas and throughout the year. When I first joined the family, the endless stream of gifts overwhelmed me. I felt like I had nothing to offer that could even come close to what they'd given me. I asked for detailed wish lists, but the lists never included more than a few small items. In twenty years, I have never been able to return their generosity.

As a Christian, I also want to give back to my Heavenly Father who gave me the greatest gift of all in His Son. I will never match His kindness either, but fortunately, God tells us exactly what He wants from us in the Bible. Near the top of His wish list is praise.

Many Christians think praise requires worship music in church. This is one way to give God praise, but there are countless others. According to Webster's 1828 Dictionary, praise is simply an expression of gratitude.

I've had some practice coming up with ways to say "Thank you" for the gifts my in-laws give me throughout the year. Cards, phone calls, being there to help, spending time with them, and writing to Great Grandma-all these things make them very happy.

It's just as simple to say "Thank you" to God. Thank Him in written, silent, or spoken prayer. Help someone, spend time in your Bible, or tell others what He's done for you. The number of ways to express gratitude to God are limited only by your imagination. Be creative and unique if you want; just praise God from your heart.

Psalm 50:23 says that "Giving thanks is a sacrifice that truly honors Me." If you'd like to honor God this Christmas, then thank Him for the gift of His only Son and for all the gifts He gives you throughout the year.

* * * * * * * *

Dear God, Thank you for the gift of Your Son Jesus, and for all the gifts you give me all year long. I will never be able to repay you, but please accept my offering of praise. Thank you! Amen.

CHRISTMAS PAST
The Legend of the Christmas Tree

"Then shall he answer them, saying, Verily I say unto you, Inasmuch as ye did it not to one of the least of these, ye did it not to me."

Matthew 25:45, WEB

In a small cottage on the borders of a forest lived a poor laborer, who gained a scanty living by cutting wood. He had a wife and two children who helped him in his work. The boy's name was Valentine, and the girl was called Mary. They were obedient, good children, and a great comfort to their parents. One winter evening, this happy little family were sitting quietly round the hearth, the snow and the wind raging outside, while they ate their supper of dry bread, when a gentle tap was heard on the window, and a childish voice cried from without:

"Oh, let me in, pray! I am a poor little child, with nothing to eat, and no home to go to, and I shall die of cold and hunger unless you let me in."

Valentine and Mary jumped up from the table and ran to open the door, saying: "Come in, poor little child! We have not much to give you, but whatever we have we will share with you."

The stranger-child came in and warmed his frozen hands and feet at the fire, and the children gave him the best they had to eat, saying: "You must be tired, too, poor child! Lie down on our bed; we can sleep on the bench for one night."

Then said the little stranger-child: "Thank God for all your kindness to me!"

So they took their little guest into their sleeping-room, laid him on the bed, covered him over, and said to each other: "How thankful we ought to be! We have warm rooms and a cozy bed, while this poor child has only heaven for his roof and the cold earth for his sleeping-place."

When their father and mother went to bed, Mary and Valentine lay quite contentedly on the bench near the fire, saying, before they fell asleep:

"The stranger-child will be so happy to-night in his warm bed!"

These kind children had not slept many hours before Mary awoke and softly whispered to her brother: "Valentine, dear, wake, and listen to the sweet music under the window."

Then Valentine rubbed his eyes and listened. It was sweet music indeed, and sounded like beautiful voices singing to the tones of a harp:

"O holy Child, we greet thee! bringing

Sweet strains of harp to aid our singing.

"Thou, holy Child, in peace art sleeping,

While we our watch without are keeping.

"Blest be the house wherein thou liest.

Happiest on earth, to heaven the highest."

The children listened, while a solemn joy filled their hearts; then they stepped softly to the window to see who might be without.

In the east was a streak of rosy dawn, and in its light they saw a group of children standing before the house, clothed in silver garments, holding golden harps in their hands. Amazed at this sight, the children were still gazing out of the window, when a light tap caused them to turn round. There stood the stranger-child before them clad in a golden dress, with a gleaming radiance round his curling hair.

"I am the little Christ-child," he said, "who wanders through the world bringing peace and happiness to good children. You took me in and cared for me when you thought me a poor child, and now you shall have my blessing for what you have done."

A fir tree grew near the house; and from this he broke a twig, which he planted in the ground, saying: "This twig shall become a tree, and shall bring forth fruit year by year for you."

No sooner had he done this than he vanished, and with him the little choir of angels. But the fir-branch grew and became a Christmas tree, and on its branches hung golden apples and silver nuts every Christmas-tide.

Such is the story told to German children concerning their beautiful Christmas trees, though we know that the real little Christ-child can never be wandering, cold and homeless, again in our world, inasmuch as he is safe in heaven by his Father's side; yet we may gather from this story the same truth which the Bible plainly tells us—that any one who helps a Christian child in distress, it will be counted unto him as if he had indeed done it unto Christ himself.

An excerpt from <u>A Budget of Christmas Tales</u>, copyright 1895 by an Anonymous writer.

SUSPENDED GIFT
by C.L. Burger

"She will give birth to a son, and you are to give him the name Jesus, because he will save his people from their sins."

Matthew 1:21, NIV

The van rumbled up the freeway exit on a cold, gray day in late November. Each time I drive over the freeway, I see the large cross on the church and feel a sense of strength and peace and I am grateful. That church was the first church to support our homeless ministry.

The Christmas gifts, donations and other supplies shifted in the back of the van as I turned the corner. Volunteers were setting up tables and chairs at another church in our faith network. The scripture and food were in place and hungry guests were waiting. Running late, I pushed on the gas pedal determined to arrive on time and unload our van.

Then I saw it. I turned on the windshield wipers to clear the mist and fog. Could it be? Somehow, the gray background of the sky blended with the support structure holding the cross. This made it appear as if God's hand alone held it up. Breathless, I blinked in disbelief at the incredible sight.

Advent is a suspended waiting—a holding by God—a breathless mystery. Advent is a season of setting the table, making ready, bringing gifts. Advent is the cross, suspended by grace alone. Advent is a time to clear away the fog of our daily lives to welcome God's *best* gift Jesus, our Lord and Savior.

✳✳✳✳✳✳✳✳

God, I thank you for giving us the gift of your Son. Help me remember that each table I set in this season of Advent and Christmas welcomes and celebrates the birth of Jesus.

EVERY GOOD GIFT
by Valerie Riese

"Whatever is good and perfect is a gift coming down to us from God our Father, who created all the lights in the heavens. He never changes or casts a shifting shadow."

James 1:17, NLT

"What can I get for my daughter for a last-minute gift for her to open Christmas morning?" I prayed to God for help.

My daughter has three rabbits, a fat one named Ioki, one with crooked ears named Penhall, and BunBun who thinks she's queen of the house. An idea popped into my head to look online. So I searched online and found the perfect gift; a cute mug with a picture of three bunnies. One of the bunnies even had crooked ears!

As I watched my teenager hug her coffee mug, I thanked God for helping me find it because it was one of her favorite gifts. The smile on her face, and knowing my little gift put it there, was one of my favorite gifts that Christmas morning.

These are the kinds of "good" and "perfect" gifts Jesus' brother referred to in James 1:17. All good gifts come from God. Your favorite fuzzy blanket– God arranged for it to land in your lap. Your pets– God created them specifically for you to love. The sunshine, the beautiful bird you spotted this morning, the flower in the side-walk– all God – all created just for you.

By reading different versions of James 1:17, I learned that "gifts" include acts of kindness. The kind stranger who jumped your stalled car–God used that person to help you just when you needed it. The little snack your husband brought home from the grocery store to cheer you up– God used him too.

When my daughter was little, we reminded her to turn around and say "Thank you" for every gift she received. Have you ever thanked God for these every-day gifts? Have you even no-ticed the Creator of the universe showers you with gifts every day?

God gives His gifts with love because He wants to see you smile, knowing that He put it there.

Don't forget to say, "Thank you."

✳✳✳✳✳✳✳✳

Dear Heavenly Father, Thank you for the gifts You give me every day. Help me to notice your expressions of love or to thank You for them. Please help me to recognize every good and perfect thing as a gift from You and to give thanks.

PEA SOUP
by Therese Kay

"Delight yourself in the LORD; And He will give you the desires of your heart."

Psalm 37:4, BSB

Several months after losing my Mom, tears still frequently visited me. As I strolled down the aisle of a grocery store, I saw a can of pea soup and lost it in the middle of the aisle. I can only imagine what the other shoppers thought as they passed by a woman clutching a can of pea soup with tears rolling down her cheeks.

Mourning the death of a loved one is hard and painful. Mourning the death of a Mom is even more so. She would no longer be sharing my earthly life. Tears and loneliness filled my days and nights for quite some time after she died.

When I saw that can of pea soup, I realized suddenly and painfully that I'd never taste my

Mom's homemade pea soup again. There were a whole lot of "never agains" that passed through my mind in rapid fire.

The can of soup was a surprisingly painful reminder that she was gone from this earthly life. I purchased that soup, went home and savored every bite. Of course, it paled in comparison to my Mom's homemade version, but with every bite, I relived memories and special times we shared. Now, every time I see a can of pea soup, rather than feeling pain, I'm reminded of special moments with her and I smile at the memories.

God can touch us so deeply through simple everyday things. I'm so grateful for the gift He gave me that day to savor those memories. Even when we don't ask, even when we may not know the desires of our heart, He does know. He is always giving us good things if we have the eyes to see.

* * * * * * * *

God, help me to see the gifts that you give me every day with a grateful and appreciative heart - even the gifts that feel painful at the time.

IN GIVING WE RECEIVE
by Cristina Vallecillo

"Every good gift and every perfect gift is from above, and cometh down from the Father of lights, with whom is no variableness, neither shadow of turning."

James 1:17, KJV

Sometimes in life, we are in such a bad place we cannot see the solution to our problem, even when it is right in front of us! Whether it be a relationship, job, financial, or health struggle, or several of them at one time. It is a normal human response to wonder, where is GOD? We need to trust and believe that GOD knows our sorrows, our struggles, and hears our cries.

I have traveled through more than a few of these moments. I have learned that GOD is the same yesterday, today, and tomorrow.

I heard this analogy on a television show. Two men were discussing how their work relationship had changed over the years. The employee said, "I am the lifeguard stand on the beach, working from a fixed position. You are the swimmer who got into the water to the left of the lifeguard stand, and over time, you drifted to the right."

That describes our relationship with GOD. We are the ones who drift away. The better question to ask is, when did I start to drift?

Amid our problems, we lose sight of the blessings our Father is still giving us. Our tunnel vision keeps our entire focus on the problem(s) and we miss the good things in life. This leads to forgetting to give thanks for our blessings of the past and thanks for those to come.

This is when we need to give thanks to GOD for His past provision and ask for His strength to sustain us through the storm. When we take that step back towards Him, He gives us what we need to survive, learn, and grow from the storm.

One way I found to weather the storm, was to stop dwelling on it and find ways to give to others. Hands down, the best cure for ending the poor me party! Giving does not always mean spending money, you may not have. There are many other ways to give another person's spirit a lift. Smile at a stranger, hold the door for the person behind you, mow your neighbor's lawn or shovel their sidewalk.

My challenge to you is to find ways to give of yourself. This will not only lift their spirits but yours too!

* * * * * * * *

Father God, Fill me with your love, for myself and those less fortunate. Increase my faith and hope in You; and my trust in the future You have in store for me! In Jesus name, Amen.

CHRISTMAS PAST
The Christmas Babe, by Margaret E. Sangster

We love to think of Bethlehem,

That little mountain town,

To which, on earth's first Christmas Day,

Our blessed Lord came down.

A lowly manger for His bed,

The cattle near in stall,

There, cradled close in Mary's arms,

He slept, the Lord of all.

If we had been in Bethlehem,

We too had hasted fain

To see the Babe whose little face

Knew neither care nor pain.

Like any little child of ours,

He came unto His own,

Through Cross and shame before Him stretched,

—

His pathway to His Throne.

If we had dwelt in Bethlehem,

We would have followed fast,

And where the Star had led our feet

Have knelt ere dawn was past.

Our gifts, our songs, our prayers had been

An offering, as He lay,

The blessed Babe of Bethlehem,

In Mary's arms that day.

Now breaks the latest Christmas Morn!

Again the angels sing,

And far and near the children throng

Their happy hymns to bring.

All heaven is stirred! All earth is glad!

For down the shining way,

The Lord who came to Bethlehem,

Comes yet, on Christmas Day.

Originally published in "A Budget of Christmas Tales"
Christian Herald, 1895

MY ANGEL IN HEAVEN
by Debra Madden

"Jesus wept"

John 11:35, KJV

The doctor came out to tell us our mother had cancer. As we stepped out of the elevator, we held each other and cried. We have always been a close family.

Mom had to have minor surgery. When she was finished, she wanted to go to dinner. I said to her, "You just had surgery." But she insisted that we go. We had a nice evening my husband, son, and I.

The next day my brother called to tell me mom was on the way to the hospital. When we arrived, she was unconscious. The doctor came in and the only words I remember were, "This woman has been Living on a Prayer." I didn't want to lose her but God gave us the time together that last evening. He spared her from all the things she would go through because of cancer. We got to celebrate her last birthday. Then she went home to be with the Lord November 14th.

I had been listening to a song "Angel On Your Shoulder" over and over as I was going through all of this with my mom. My sister-in-law gave me a necklace, not knowing anything about the song. I opened it and there was a heart with my mom's picture etched on it and on the back was engraved "angel watching over you."

Christmas was not the same without mom. I thank God for the special memories he gave me that year.

Christmas is a time of joy and celebration for most families.

For many, who are alone or have recently lost a loved one, it's the hardest times of the year. Ask God what you can do to help someone who is hurting. It's a great time to reach out and show someone the love of Christ.

I wrote this song for my mom. I hope it will bring comfort to those that are having a hard Christmas this year.

Be Still

Vs. 1 I will walk with you through the darkest night.

I will give you peace to the morning Light.

I will carry you when you feel alone.

I will calm your heart though the storms rage on.

Chorus:

Be still and know that I am God

Be still and know that I am God

Be still and know that I am God and I will carry you

Vs. 2 I know the pain you feel don't turn and run away

I know just what you need just trust in me and pray

I know your strength is gone you feel you can't go on

But I am here for you with open arms so strong

Chorus:

Vs. 3 I know the fears you feel I see the tears you cry

I even understand when you asked me why

Child I love you more than words could ever say don't ever doubt my love it's here for you each day.

Chorus:

* * * * * * * *

Dear God, Please help me to feel your love and comfort - a comfort no one else can give.

THE GOSPEL — PAY IT FORWARD
by Debi Flory

> *"Heal the sick raise the dead, cleanse lepers, cast out demons. You received without paying, give without pay."*
>
> *Matthew 10:8, ESV*

Who was the first to pay it forward? As Christians, it surely seems it was God, sending his Son to pay for our sins before we were even born.

The season of advent finds me embracing Joseph and Mary and their selfless gift of obedience. I am in awe of their willingness to give more than they knew they had. Joseph taught us the gift of humility. He said "Yes" to the Lord's direction to wed Mary, knowing he was not the father of the child she carried. He showed amazing grace as a loving stepfather to Jesus. Joseph, in humility, chose unconditional love over cultural traditions vs marrying his beloved Mary.

Mary gifted us with the example of humble servant-hood, blessed obedience, and the opportunity to understand her dance with grief and joy. There is no way to compare the gift of salvation with Mary's call to carry and deliver the gospel in the flesh. Still, there is no way to compare that blessing with the humility and unconditional love of our Lord's ultimate sacrifice.

We so often find ourselves focused on the best gift of the season for family and friends. I marvel at the opportunity we have to keep paying it forward the way Mary and Joseph so lovingly and selflessly did.

We can turn Advent into the opportunity to pay forward the story of the gospel to others, to pay forward the miracle of Christ's gift to the world. In every Christmas carol we sing, with every kindness we show, with every act of grace we show, we pay forward the love of Jesus to others.

Jesus came in a lowly manger, naked and vulnerable to bring a message of sacrificial love to those who would hear. Mary and Joseph remained in the background while they co-authored the greatest story ever told. They are heroes of mine. I am so grateful for their humble gifts to the world. Mary carried the Gospel, Joseph believed she carried the Gospel and the Gospel brought Joy to the World.

****

Lord, help me carry the Gospel all Christmas season so that others may carry it too. Amen.

THE ULTIMATE GIFT
by Marné Kleinhans

"I have satiated the weary soul, and I have replenished every sorrowful soul".

Jeremiah 31:25, KJV

Do you feel more exhausted than festive? I can relate. Lack of inspiration and energy is a reality for many of us special needs parents. Society is unable to accept your child, who has the biggest needs, but also the biggest potential. This is emotionally draining. Some of us are tired, trying to make ends meet, fighting for survival in a world that revolves around the economy. Perhaps we're shattered after reading the newspaper or tuning in to a news broadcast. We may be scared of what tomorrow might bring. We might have health challenges or grieving the death of a loved one.

God sees, hears and knows everything. He saw our isolation as parents. He heard our prayers. He knew what we were facing every day. We thought we were without help and hope. Fortunately, we serve an Almighty Father. He not only gave us His son but also gave us the promise that He will restore the tired and weary.

If we look upon the mountain we are facing, He is there to answer our call. If we look at the human impossible challenge, He is there to comfort us. He was our salvation by sending others as instruments in His hands. He gave us others to be there for us emotionally, to help us financially, to stand in prayer with us and to help us restore our faith and dignity.

Some of us push ourselves to a point of overwhelm to get loved ones the perfect gift. Yet, the one who loves us the most already has the perfect gift to offer, the gift of rest and inner peace. Our Father is an abundant giver. He gives rest to those who come to him. He gives assurance that we, the tired, will find peace and restoration for our weary souls.

Perhaps we should not focus on giving the ultimate gift to others but focus on the gifts we already have received in unlimited abundance. Then we will be able to give from the heart, give a gift that touches others. If we have inner peace, our peace will flow onto the souls of our loved ones. For inner peace is one of the greatest gifts there is.

After Christmas, the guests have gone home, the wrapping paper has been cleared and the festive music has faded in the background. In the stillness of the night, I am not scared of the reality I have to face again. I have received the greatest gift of all, the gift of peace and assurance that he will restore my weary soul. I do not have to worry about what tomorrow might bring.

* * * * * * * *

Lord, we thank you for being our salvation. We thank you for giving us the ultimate gifts, no money can buy. We thank you in the abundance that you give us what we need. All glory to our Father who restores our weary souls.

BRINGING JOY TO THE WORLD
by Cristina Vallecillo

"A generous person will prosper; whoever refreshes others will be refreshed."

Proverbs 11:25, NIV

When you learn that the gift you have decided to give, has a special meaning to the one to whom you are giving, it sets the heart to quivering.

There is a joy and excitement, which the heart feels when the happiness of the recipient is revealed.

If the weight of your world is pulling you down, giving of yourself brings some perspective and helps turn things around.

Be on the lookout for things you can do. Whatever it is, will be a help to them and a benefit to you.

The more you experience this awesome phenomenon called giving, it will amaze you at how much better and brighter is your everyday living.

The more joy to the world you are bringing, the more your heart feels like singing!

I am not one to do and tell. I am making an exception in this case, to share the jaw-dropping event, which happened this past summer. I want this story to be a testament to the Amazing God of ours! The above poem came about from that event.

One day as I was balancing my checkbook, I realized my Pay It Forward Fund had more of a balance than it should. This meant I was not doing a very good job of paying it forward. Suddenly the familiar quiet voice of God said to me, "Giving is not just for Christmas." We had a short conversation about this. Then the quiet voice said, "What about a day at the Water Park for the family you had adopted before at Christmas?"

I contacted the woman who is the go-between the family and me and left a message. When she got back to me, I told her the message I received and what I had in mind. She said she would contact the family and get back to me.

A few weeks went by before she called me back. She said the family was thrilled and excited! Then she said, "Before the father became disabled, he helped build the Water Park." To say that this stunned me is a gross understatement! All I kept thinking was nobody but God could have put this together!

I am happy to report they all had a great time!

* * * * * * * *

Heavenly Father, I hope that your words will inspire the desire in many hearts to give of themselves this year. I pray that all will feel your presence and your quiet voice they will hear. May thy will be done and may many experience some unexpected fun. In Jesus name. Amen.

CHRISTMAS PAST
The Osborne's Christmas

"That isn't what I mean," said Cousin Myra. "How much Christmas do you suppose those little Rolands down there in the hollow have? Or Sammy Abbott with his lame back? Or French Joe's family over the hill? If you have too much Christmas, why don't you give some to them?"

The Osbornes looked at each other. This was a new idea.

"How could we do it?" asked Ida.

Whereupon they had a consultation. Cousin Myra explained her plan, and the Osbornes grew enthusiastic over it. Even Frank forgot that he was supposed to be wearing a cynical sneer.

"I move we do it, Osbornes," said he.

"If Father and Mother are willing," said Ida.

"Won't it be jolly!" exclaimed the twins.

"Well, rather," said Darby scornfully. He did not mean to be scornful. He had heard Frank saying the same words in the same tone, and thought it signified approval.

Cousin Myra had a talk with Father and Mother Osborne that night, and found them heartily in sympathy with her plans.

For the next week the Osbornes were agog with excitement and interest. At first Cousin Myra made the suggestions, but their enthusiasm soon outstripped her, and they thought out things for themselves. Never did a week pass so quickly. And the Osbornes had never had such fun, either.

Christmas morning there was not a single present given or received at "The Firs" except those which Cousin Myra and Mr. and Mrs. Osborne gave to each other. The junior Osbornes had asked that the money which their parents had planned to spend in presents for them be given to them the previous week; and given it was, without a word.

The uncles and aunts arrived in due time, but not with them was the junior Osbornes' concern. They were the guests of Mr. and Mrs. Osborne. The junior Osbornes were having a Christmas dinner party of their own. In the small dining room a table was spread and loaded with good things. Ida and the twins cooked that dinner all by themselves. To be sure, Cousin Myra had helped some, and Frank and Darby had stoned all the raisins and helped pull the home-made candy; and all together they had decorated the small dining room royally with Christmas greens.

Then their guests came. First, all the little Rolands from the Hollow arrived—seven in all, with very red, shining faces and not a word to say for themselves, so shy were they. Then came a troop from French Joe's—four black-eyed lads, who never knew what shyness meant. Frank drove down to the village in the cutter and brought lame Sammy back with him, and soon after the last guest arrived—little Tillie Mather, who was Miss Rankin's "orphan 'sylum girl" from over the road. Everybody knew that Miss Rankin never kept Christmas. She did not believe in it, she said, but she did not prevent Tillie from going to the Osbornes' dinner party.

Just at first the guests were a little stiff and unsocial; but they soon got acquainted, and so jolly was Cousin Myra—who had her dinner with the children in preference to the grown-ups —and so friendly the junior Osbornes, that all stiffness vanished. What a merry dinner it was!

What peals of laughter went up, reaching to the big dining room across the hall, where the grown-ups sat in rather solemn state. And how those guests did eat and frankly enjoy the good things before them! How nicely they all behaved, even to the French Joes! Myra had secretly been a little dubious about those four mischievous-looking lads, but their manners were quite flawless. Mrs. French Joe had been drilling them for three days—ever since they had been invited to "de Chrismus dinner at de beeg house."

After the merry dinner was over, the junior Osbornes brought in a Christmas tree, loaded with presents. They had bought them with the money that Mr. and Mrs. Osborne had meant for their own presents, and a splendid assortment they were. All the French-Joe boys got a pair of skates apiece, and Sammy a set of beautiful books, and Tillie was made supremely happy with a big wax doll. Every little Roland got just what his or her small heart had been longing for. Besides, there were nuts and candies galore.

Then Frank hitched up his pony again, but this time into a great pung sleigh, and the junior Osbornes took their guests for a sleigh-drive, chaperoned by Cousin Myra. It was just dusk when they got back, having driven the Rolands and the French Joes and Sammy and Tillie to their respective homes.

"This has been the jolliest Christmas I ever spent," said Frank, emphatically.

"I thought we were just going to give the others a good time, but it was they who gave it to us," said Ida.

"Weren't the French Joes jolly?" giggled the twins. "Such cute speeches as they would make!"

"Me and Teddy Roland are going to be chums after this," announced Darby. "He's an inch taller than me, but I'm wider."

That night Frank and Ida and Cousin Myra had a little talk after the smaller Osbornes had been haled off to bed.

"We're not going to stop with Christmas, Cousin Myra," said Frank, at the end of it. "We're just going to keep on through the year. We've never had such a delightful old Christmas before."

"You've learned the secret of happiness," said Cousin Myra gently.

And the Osbornes understood what she meant.

Excerpt from the book Lucy Maud Montgomery Short Stories, 1902 to 1903. Copyright expired.

GOD WITH US
by Valerie Riese

"Look! The virgin will conceive a child! She will give birth to a son, and they will call him Immanuel, which means 'God is with us.'"

Matthew 1:23, NLT

God assigned names to many people in the Bible. Often the name revealed the very purpose for which the person was born. For example, in Genesis 17:5, God changed Abram's name to "Abraham", which means "father of a multitude. Abraham would be the great-grandfather of the 12 tribes of Israel. Also, God named King David's son "Solomon," which means "peace" in Hebrew. Indeed, King Solomon's reign was long and peaceful.

So, when God announced His own human birth, what name did He give Himself? The first name revealed for God made flesh was "Immanuel," which means, "God is with us." Jesus' purpose, as revealed by His name, is to be *with* us.

We know His Spirit lives inside us, but how often do you spend quality time just being *with* God? Have you praised Him in song or prayer lately - without asking for anything? Did you thank Him for the sunrise today? The Word *is* God, so I'm sure He'd be thrilled to meet you in your Bible.

God also wants us to be with each other, especially to support the sick and hurting. In Matthew 25:31-46, Jesus said when we look after the sick and visit prisoners; it's the same as though we'd been there for Him. So, reach out with a text, a card, a phone call, or a visit to a friend, family member, or stranger.

God came to be with you because you are important to Him. He gave you the gift of Himself as a baby in a manger, and ultimately His very Spirit living inside you.

Ask God what He'd like to do together today. Don't be late, and don't forget. After all, He came all the way from Heaven to be with you.

****

Dear Heavenly Father, Thank you for coming to be with us. Please ignite a desire for your company in my heart and lead me to draw near to you. Amen

THE GIFT OF ENCOURAGEMENT
by Therese Kay

"Therefore encourage one another and build each other up, just as in fact you are doing."

1 Thessalonians 5:11, NIV

I spotted the biggest present under the tree that year and it was for me! I couldn't wait to open it when I saw it Christmas morning! This one wasn't from Santa but from my folks. They wanted to be sure to get credit for this one!

When it was finally my turn to choose a gift to unwrap, I went straight to that one, eager to see what was inside. I was baffled as I tore off the paper and found a big cardboard "under-the-bed" box.

What I found inside was one of the best gifts I ever received. I found drawing paper, charcoal, pastels, watercolors, instruction booklets, scissors, clay, paintbrushes. Name an art supply that a young child would want, and it was probably in there.

While my sisters enjoyed sports, I enjoyed reading, writing, and creating. I was definitely the odd one out of my siblings. I didn't simply dislike sports--I was exceptionally bad at them. I wanted to be a poet or an artist when I grew up. My parents not only accepted this but also embraced it and encouraged it.

The actual art supplies in my special box were amazing, but the bigger and better gift was to be encouraged to be me! Even when my mind changed later on in childhood and I wanted to be a wildlife biologist and outdoor woman "extraordinaire." They gave me gift subscriptions to *National Wildlife* and *Outdoor Life*. Wherever my imagination took my future, my parents were there to encourage me and cheer me on.

The art supplies have long been used up and the magazines have been recycled but the encouragement has lasted my whole life. I embraced the creativity that was encouraged in me as a child. Now, as I was encouraged, I've also been given the gift of encouraging others.

As you plan your gifts, ask how you can encourage the recipients. What makes them unique and special? How can you recognized and celebrate that with the gift you give?

****

Dear Lord, help me to encourage others, as I was encouraged. Help me to encourage others to be the person God created them to be and celebrate their uniqueness.

BEING A FRIEND
by Marné Kleinhans

"So he ran on ahead and climbed a sycamore tree to see Him, since Jesus was about to pass that way. When Jesus came to that place, He looked up and said, "Zacchaeus, hurry down, for I must stay at your house today."

Luke 19:1-5, NLT

Zacchaeus was a man with few friends, and with a lot of judgment of character against him. His deeds were not acceptable to society, his true worthiness unknown to humanity. Yet, like all of us, he longed for acceptance and love from his nearest.

When Jesus went home with Zacchaeus, the masses were full of judgment and insults. To them it was not acceptable that an honorable man like Jesus would be a guest of a dishonest man like Zacchaeus. Jesus looked past the judgment. He saw Zacchaeus's heart. He knew there was good in Him. He even knew his name.

One of the greatest gifts we can receive is the gift of having a friend. Someone who accepts you for who you are without judging or prejudice. Someone who wants to build a relationship with you, no matter what. Some of my most treasured possessions are gifts received from friends. But the gifts that made the greatest impact on my life are the friends who came into my life and made a difference, simply by being there for me.

I can almost imagine my life as a big Christmas tree and my friends are the presents underneath. Each one individually unique. Yet, all of them have one big purpose, making the bigger picture of my life beautiful, enriching it in many ways. When my burdens feel too heavy to carry alone, I know I have support. When I need wisdom and direction in life, I know where to turn to. When I need to laugh and play, I have friends to share my time with. My friends are my most valued gifts.

By merely having a relationship with Zacchaeus, Jesus changed his life forever. Perhaps Jesus is also trying to get our attention to interact with people we never would think of doing so. The neighbor who annoys us, the cleaner at work, that mom at school who we just can't seem to like... Perhaps it is them, who God is using through their traits, to get our attention. We can make a difference in their lives, by being their friend.

****

Father, help me to see the best in everyone, just like you do. So that I too can make a difference in the lives of others by enriching their lives with friendship.

HE GAVE THE LITTLE HE HAD
by Sharon Rose Gibson

"He who gives to the poor lends to the Lord and He will reward you for what you have done."

Proverbs 19:17, NIV

"Stop, wait a minute. I want to help this woman," I shouted to my family who walked on ahead of me on the streets of Sao Paulo, Brazil. We had taken the bus downtown to the court-house to meet with the social workers.

We had adopted Alex from a severe poverty situation in Brazil when he was fifteen. After he grew up and graduated from a local university, we sat on the couch one day visiting. "Mom, I know I could stay here in the USA and buy a nice house and car. But what I want to do is to give my brother and sisters trapped in poverty, the same opportunities I had."

After many years and attempts to bring them here, we were in Brazil to go through the formidable legal process. We decided to adopt Alex's siblings, seventeen-year-old Michelle, thirteen-year-old Ingrid, and twelve-year-old Michael. We had finished our court appointment and we were on the way to catch the bus to the apartment where we were staying.

I spotted a woman sitting on the dirty sidewalk with a tin can by her side. She had a baby cradled in her arms and a little boy and girl in dirty clothes playing beside her. My heart moved with deep compassion. Was it the look of sadness and despair in her eyes as she sought to get food to feed her little ones? I don't know. I simply knew I had to help her even if it was only for one meal that day.

I walked over to the nearest food stand to purchase some sandwiches and drinks. As I stood there, twelve-year-old Michael came up behind me and handed me a bill, the equivalent of a dollar. "Here mom," he said quietly, "I want to help."

Tears sprang to my eyes as I knew Michael didn't have much himself. Yet he knew what it was like to be in that situation. He wanted to take the little he had to help someone in a worse condition.

As I walked away that day and for days after, I prayed that somehow God would make a way for her to get out of that situation.

As I reflect on this touching incident during the Christmas season, those in need come to mind. Jesus gave it all and He cares deeply about the poor. We honor Him when we give to them. We may not be able to do a lot but that doesn't have to stop us from giving the little we have.

****

Lord, help us be more aware of how we can share your good news and generosity during this celebration of your birth. Show us the little we can do during this season to give to those in need and to honor you.

CHRISTMAS PAST
What Christmas is as We Grow Older,
by Charles Dickens

Therefore, as we grow older, let us be more thankful that the circle of our Christmas associations and of the lessons that they bring, expands! Let us welcome every one of them, and summon them to take their places by the Christmas hearth.

Welcome, old aspirations, glittering creatures of an ardent fancy, to your shelter underneath the holly! We know you, and have not outlived you yet. Welcome, old projects and old loves, however fleeting, to your nooks among the steadier lights that burn around us. Welcome, all that was ever real to our hearts; and for the earnestness that made you real, thanks to Heaven! Do we build no Christmas castles in the clouds now? Let our thoughts, fluttering like butterflies among these flowers of children, bear witness! Before this boy, there stretches out a Future, brighter than we ever looked on in our old romantic time, but bright with honour and with truth. Around this little head on which the sunny curls lie heaped, the graces sport, as prettily, as airily, as when there was no scythe within the reach of Time to shear away the curls of our first-love. Upon another girl's face near it— placider but smiling bright—a quiet and contented little face, we see Home fairly written. Shining from the word, as rays shine from a star, we see how, when our graves are old, other hopes than ours are young, other hearts than ours are moved; how other ways are smoothed; how other happiness blooms, ripens, and decays—no, not decays, for other homes and other bands of children, not yet in being nor for ages yet to be, arise, and bloom and ripen to the end of all!

Welcome, everything! Welcome, alike what has been, and what never was, and what we hope may be, to your shelter underneath the holly, to your places round the Christmas fire, where what is sits open-hearted! In yonder shadow, do we see obtruding furtively upon the blaze, an enemy's face? By Christmas Day we do forgive him! If the injury he has done us may admit of such companionship, let him come here and take his place. If otherwise, unhappily, let him go hence, assured that we will never injure nor accuse him.

On this day we shut out Nothing!

Excerpt from <u>A Budget of Christmas Tales</u> by Charles Dickens and others, copyright 1895

LOVE OTHERS
by Debra Madden

"This is my commandment, that ye love one another as I have loved you."

John 15:12, KJV

A family friend asked me to sing at a funeral he was officiating. We had never met the woman who had asked us to come and share in the service. She walked up to us and introduced herself. "I am so sorry, but I do not have the finances to pay you." We assured her we were there to be a blessing and nothing else.

I believe we need to intentionally look for ways that we can bless and love others, not looking for anything in return. God said to put others before ourselves.

God had laid it on my heart to make a cake in the shape of a cross for the woman. After the funeral I handed the cake to someone to give to her and left.

After some time, I received a card in the mail from the woman. She thanked me and told me how much it touched her heart that I had made the cake for her. She had enclosed a check in the card.

We are called to love others. It's easy to love the people that love us and are good to us. But It can be very challenging to love those that are difficult and hurtful. We can't forget that God loves us even at our worst.

My husband was on his way to work one day. He stopped for breakfast. As he pulled through the drive-through, there was a vehicle with two men inside. They honked their horn and yelled at my husband. They felt that he had jumped in front of them. Out of frustration, my husband started yelling back at them.

When my husband pulled up, the young man at the window of the restaurant heard the commotion. He knew it upset my husband. He tried to defuse the situation. The young man's comment reminded my husband that we are to love others even when it's hard.

God brought it to my husband's mind to pay for their order. My husband asked the guy at the window to give them a message, "Tell them there's a lot going on in the world today and we need to get along with each other." As my husband drove off the young man at the window said, "Have a blessed day."

God wants to use us to show his love to the world. God can do mighty things when we choose to love even when it's undeserved and difficult. It's a choice we have to make, and God will always be right by our side to give us the help we need. There is a blessing in our obedience to love others.

* * * * * * * *

Father, fill us with your love for others. Help us let go quickly when people hurt and offend us. Open our eyes to the many opportunities you give us each day to show your love to the people around us. In Jesus name, Amen.

PRAISE IN BROKEN PIECES
by Debi Flory

"God, pick up the pieces. Put me back to-gether again. You are my praise!"

Jeremiah 17:14, KJV

We took a devastating hit during the financial recession. We scrambled for almost a year to catch our breath, pick ourselves up and walk again. Now, it was the Christmas season and my world had changed. We moved to Oregon, a place of refuge, fully expecting to recover financially and spiritually once our home sold. But the house did not sell. Everything came to a screeching halt. Christmas would come, regardless.

The usual pile of gifts for my large blended family could not be the usual carefree fun this year. This year would be different. I felt sad and depressed that I could not be a very good Santa this year. I let the circumstances of my life overshadow my understanding of the true meaning of Christmas. So, I prayed.

God encouraged me to stay with the Christmas message of love and think about what I could do, not what I couldn't. An artist, new to stained glass mosaic, I decided to mosaic everyone a gift. I found a local source of free scrap glass from local stained-glass artists. I took what little Christmas cash I had and bought window frames and picture frames. I started creating from all the discarded, donated "orphan" pieces of glass. I love stained glass, even the broken pieces. There is beauty in every single piece.

As I layered every piece, I found myself in meditation and prayer over each child.

The pieces became little prayers as I thought about the gifts and challenges each child faced out in the world on their own. The healing began for me. My heart began to empty of my own grief and fill with the love and appreciation for my children. I put together the beautiful broken pieces of glass to create an entirely new piece. All the broken pieces were more beautiful and brilliant than the original single sheet of glass.

My gift came from God that year. With every piece of glass and every prayer, God began piecing me back together. He reminded me that I would be more beautiful of heart, more brilliant in spirit and more willing to praise Him in the moment.

As Pastor Wendy Olson says, *"Praise God, whose mode of operation is to take the tiny bits you hold in your hands and heart and stir them into the mix Jesus Christ is concocting."*

* * * * * * * *

How has God stepped in to pick up the pieces and put you back together again?

GIFT FROM A CHILD

by C.L. Burger

"For I do not do the good I want to do, but the evil I do not want to do-this I keep on doing."

Romans 7:19, NIV

I heard the pat, pat, pat of little feet snugly wrapped in Christmas footie pajamas. My granddaughter stood next to our Christmas tree and reached out with her tiny hand. At three years old, the colorful lights, shiny round ornaments and especially the glass angels up high in the tree captivated her. Her big brown eyes reflected in the gold ball hanging from the branch closest to her sweet face.

"You can look with your eyes, but please don't touch the ornaments."

My granddaughter smiled. "Okay Grandma, I'll just look and stay right here." I turned to go back into the kitchen and heard the inevitable crash. Tears welled up in her eyes. "I didn't mean to Grandma, I'm sorry." The gold ornament had shattered around her feet. I hugged her and told her it was okay, but reminded her (again) to look with her eyes and to follow Grandma's directions. She shrugged her shoulders and with an impish grin said, "I don't know why I did that, I guess that's just the way I am."

My granddaughter gave me a special gift that night. Through a little child, I had a living reminder of the lesson in Romans 7:19. I realized I was much like my granddaughter in my Heavenly Father's eyes when I ignore His warnings and excuse my disobedience with, "That's just the way I am." Yet with mercy, love, and forgiveness, He hugs me and gives me another chance to show him I can follow His ways.

* * * * * * * *

Lord, help me follow your ways and not make excuses when I disobey. Thank you for loving and forgiving me even when I don't always listen.

THE WONDER OF CHRISTMAS
by Cristina Vallecillo

"All this is for your benefit, so that the grace that is reaching more and more people may cause thanksgiving to overflow to the glory of God."

2 Corinthians 4:15, NIV

A teacher asked a group of students to list what they thought were the present-day Seven Wonders of the World. Though there was some disagreement, the following got the most votes:

1. Egypt's Great Pyramids
2. Taj Mahal
3. Grand Canyon
4. Panama Canal
5. Empire State Building
6. St. Peter's Basilica
7. China's Great Wall

While gathering the votes, the teacher noted that one student hadn't turned in her paper yet. She asked the girl if she was having trouble with her list.

The girl replied, "Yes, a little. I couldn't quite decide because there are so many." The teacher said, "Tell us what you have, and maybe we can help."

The girl hesitated, then read, "I think the Seven Wonders of the World are:

1. to See
2. to Taste
3. to Touch
4. to Hear

She hesitated a little, and then added,

5. to Feel
6. to Laugh
7. and to Love

The room was so full of silence you could've heard a pin drop. Those things we overlook as simple and "ordinary" are truly wondrous. This is a gentle reminder that we cannot buy the most precious things in life. God gave them to us.

— Author: Unknown

I read this story and it reminded me of how much we take for granted, instead of expressing gratitude.

Many years back, I was channel surfing one morning and came to a woman preacher. She was the first I had ever seen, so I stopped to listen for a while. As I listened, I knew I was experiencing a God Nod; it was as if Joyce Meyer was speaking to me.

Joyce was talking about having an attitude of gratitude. She said, "Everyone, and I mean everyone, can find at least one thing to be grateful for every day!" That hit home and made me realize it had been quite a while since I had given thanks to GOD for anything.

Joyce also said something else that has stuck with me over the years, especially when I hit a bump in the road of life. She said, "Lord, I am not where I want to be, but thank God, I'm not where I used to be"

Since that long-ago day, I thank God daily for the blessings and lessons in my life. No coincidence here that over the years, the list has grown well beyond the list of three things with which I started.

May the wonder of Christmas and all it represents be the focus of your celebration!

* * * * * * * *

Father, I pray that everyone reading this gives You thanks and praise daily for the gift of your Son, JESUS CHRIST, our Redeemer and Savior. There has never been nor ever will be any greater gift than this! Amen.

GIVING THOUGHTS

Your open hand has more power than your clenched fist.

The Three Types of Givers

The Flint - You must hammer and beg this person. When you do get something, it is sparks and chips.

The Sponge - To get something from the sponge you must squeeze and apply pressure. The more pressure the more you get. But, it's not given with a willing heart.

The Honeycomb - The honeycomb overflows with sweetness and gives without asking

You can give without loving, but you can't love without giving.

It's not what we get that measures the success of our life, but rather what we give.

If you want to have a **rich life**, then give your life.

If you want to have a **poor life**, then grasp and hold onto things.

If you want an **abundant life**, then scatter seeds abundantly.

If you want to have a **needy life**, then hoard all your blessings.

A NEW YEAR

Little children are usually snug in bed when the first holiday of the year arrives. It comes at midnight when all is dark out of doors. Sometimes the weather is very cold, here in England, with snow upon the ground; and as it nears midnight on the 31st December there is a great silence beneath the stars. The children are in bed; but in most homes there are grown-up people— fathers, mothers, uncles or aunts—who sit late and watch the clock. They watch; and when the clock strikes twelve they know that the first day of the New Year has arrived.

Then it is no longer silent out of doors. The bells are ringing loudly, and ringing merrily; they are ringing a welcome to the Stranger. So the grown-up people, who have been watching the clock, rise up smiling and wish each other a Happy New Year. The father says to the mother: "I wish you a Happy New Year, my dear," and in saying this they shake hands,[4] and kiss each other. Then the mother, if she has children in bed, goes upstairs. They are all asleep; so she does not waken them. She simply kisses them, each one, and smiles as she whispers: "A Happy New Year to all of you, my dears." That is how the New Year arrives in England. In Scotland there is more ceremony. There it used to be the custom for the whole household to sit up till twelve o'clock and bring in the New Year with singing and frolic. But that custom is dying out.

You children, I hope, get to know about the New Year in the morning. You find that everybody is looking happy, and wishing happiness to other people. Even although the sun is not shining there is brightness in the house and in the street. People when they meet shake hands and joke and laugh. Your aunt will give you a good hug, and more than likely your uncle will put his hand into his pocket and give you something; something round and bright; something that will make you smile. Then you learn that the New Year brings gifts as well as gladness.

But nowadays the giving of presents is not so common as it used to be. Far back in English history the grown-up people gave each other gifts on New Year's Day, and some of these gifts were very beautiful and very costly. Diamond necklaces, gold caskets, jewelled swords, embroidered mantles—these were the kind of gifts which rich people gave to each other at the feast of the New Year. Our English Kings and Queens, in the old days, received many such precious gifts. Queen Elizabeth got so many valuable presents in this way that a list of them was kept upon parchment, and in the history books it may still be read.

This custom of giving rich presents to rich people on New Year's Day exists no longer in England; and that is well. For in many cases these costly gifts were given not from kindness but from selfishness; the gift-givers wanted some favour in return. Now, it is an ill thing to begin a New Year with a spirit of greediness. None of you children, I am sure, will do so.

Be thankful that you have got the gift of another New Year's Day. It is the first clean page of a fine new book in which you can write just what you please. Write something cheerful; and see to it that there are no blots.

****

Dear Lord, on the cusp of this fresh new year, please help me to find ways to enrich the lives of others. Amen.

Excerpt from Holidays and Happy Days by Hamish Hendry, copyright 1901

ABOUT THE AUTHORS

C.L. Burger is an author, speaker, blogger and Spiritual Director. Cindy offers the light of God's hope through her Memoir, Once in a Lullaby: My Journey Home, her blog ministry and her online spiritual direction practice at Holy Listening.com. She has three grown children and four granddaughters. She and her husband live in California where they serve as staff for their large Maine Coon cat. You can find Cindy at www.clburgerlullabyjourney.blog, www.holylistening.com or her C.L. Burger Facebook Page

Debi Flory, a Spiritual Director with Holy Listening and owner of Spirit in the Arts retreat center on the Oregon coast, incorporates contemplative art, comedy and music to companion others on the path to joy. She's proud of her incredible blended family. Debi can be reached at HolyListening.com or her retreat center at www.spiritinthearts.com. Follow her blog at www.-peanutbutterpicklesandmayo.com.

Sharon Rose Gibson has a passion to empower you to Write Your Story NOW at 15minutewriter.com. She's been published in bestselling books such as the Chicken Soup series and authored three books. She recently published, "How to Write Your Story NOW - Writing Skills to Captivate Your Reader." Her missionary parents raised her in Africa, and she's adopted seven teenagers from poverty backgrounds.

Therese Kay is a photographer, writer, and lover of God from Lynn, MA. When not taking pictures, you can find her writing or editing photos. She is author of Meeting God through Art: Visio Divina and co-author of Messages from God: An Illuminated Devotional. Learn more about her at www.ThereseKay.com

Marné Kleinhans is a special needs activist, mother, farmer's wife and blogger. When she is not writing, she assists the Brain Child Fund in supporting other special needs families across Africa. Her award-nominated blog, www.raisingmyautisticfarmer.wordpress.com, inspires many to see the breakthrough in every breakdown.

Debra L Madden is a writer, singer, poet. She loves to share her testimony at women's gatherings. Her passion is to help women find freedom and God's purpose for their life. She lives in Virginia with her husband and son. Contact her at Debra L Madden Facebook, @spiritledwords orwww.facebook.com/Spiritledwords

Valerie Riese lives in Wisconsin with her husband, daughter, three rabbits, and a guinea pig. After suffering years of debilitating anxiety, she now has a passion to help women overcome anxiety through faith on her blog VictoryThroughSurrender.com. She is also a regular contributor and prayer team liaison on CandidlyChristian.com.

Kathleen Schwab is a lifelong lover of God, a literature teacher, a writer, and a wife and mother. She grew up learning about God by reading the popular children's series *The Bible Story*. In partnership with photographer Therese Kay, Kathleen is the author of Messages from God: An Illuminated Devotional, a five-week full color devotional inspired by the illuminated manuscripts of the Middle Ages.

Cristina Vallecillo has written faith-based poetry since 2003. For four years she's shared "A Sunday Afternoon Message" on her Facebook Wall. She's launched a Blog called "With HIS Abundant Grace" and is working on an E-book which will publish soon. Learn more about Cristina at WithHISAbundantGrace.com

When she's not sweeping dog hair, cooking, or doodling on paper, **Kim C. Steadman** writes and mentors authors. She is a freelance writer, teacher and ministers alongside her family in Grand Prairie, TX. Her books include prayer journals and children's books. Follow her prayerful writing world at KimSteadman.com. Kim has a heart and passion to encourage Christians of all ages to write the words in their hearts and minds. WriteMore-WriteNow.com is her faith based online writing club.

PART 2: LINED JOURNAL PAGES

The next section contains 100 lined pages for writing Bible scripture, your thoughts and prayers as you read through your daily devotional. These pages are ideal for reflections, journal writing or Bible study while you read this devotional.